mommy

mama

daddy

papa

boy

nen

girl

nena

1 one

un

2 two

dos

3 three

tres

4 four

quatre

5

five

cinc

6

six

sis

7

seven

set

8

eight

vuit

9

nine

nou

10

ten

deu

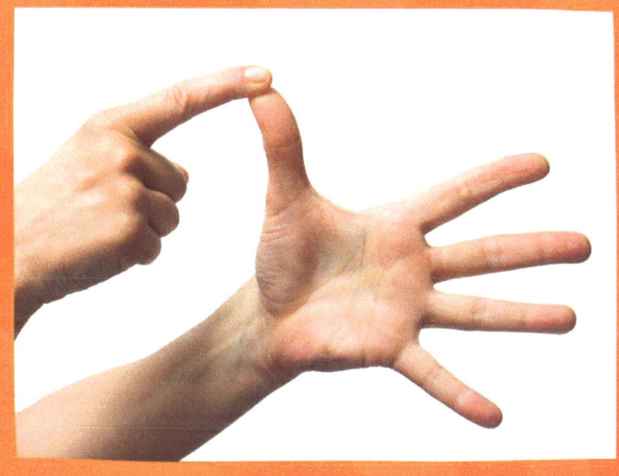

count

comptar

write

escriure

draw

dibuixar

paint

pintar

circle

cercle

square

quadrat

rectangle

rectangle

triangle

triangle

star

estrella

black

negre

white

blanc

brown

marró

red

vermell

blue

blau

yellow

groc

green

verd

purple

violat

gray

gris

orange

taronja

pink

rosa

apple

poma

banana

plàtan

pineapple

pinya

watermelon

síndria

pear

pera

grapes

raïm

mango

mango

peach

préssec

strawberry

maduixa

cherry

cirera

orange

taronja

coconut

coco

lemon

llimona

mushroom

bolet

corn

blat de moro

tomato

tomàquet

pumpkin

carbassa

cucumber

cogombre

carrot

pastanaga

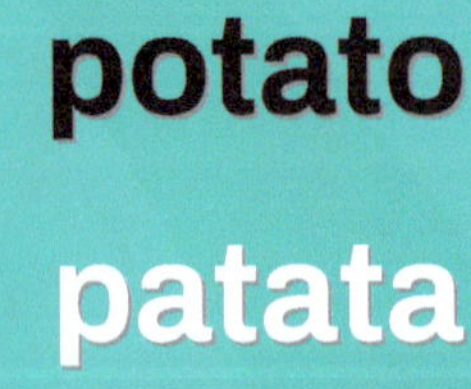

potato

patata

zucchini

carbassó

spinach

espinacs

cauliflower

coliflor

egg

ou

plate

plat

spoon

cullera

knife

ganivet

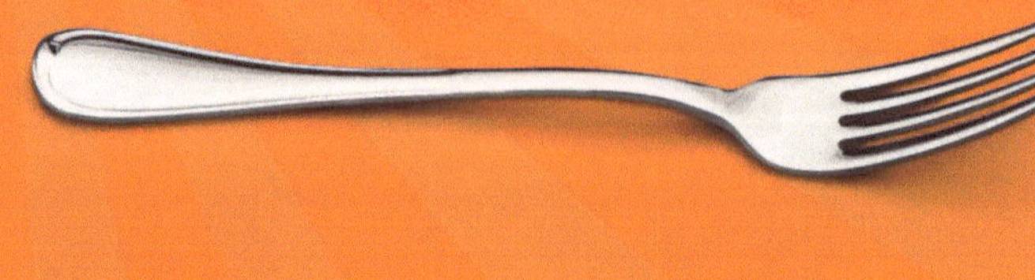

fork

forquilla

cake

pastís

baby bottle

biberó

candies

llaminadures

cheese

formatge

drink

beure

eat

menjar

hot

calent

cold

fred

small

petit

big

gran

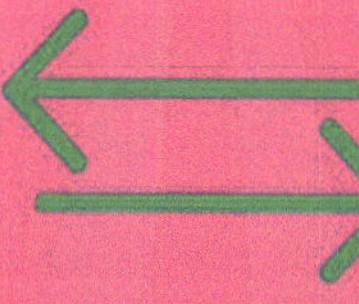
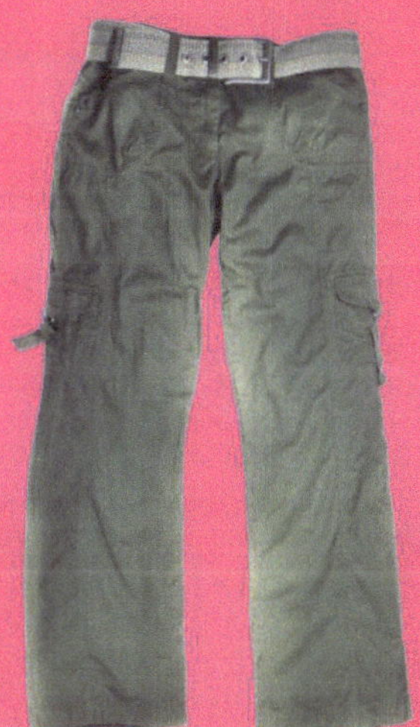

short

curt

long

llarg

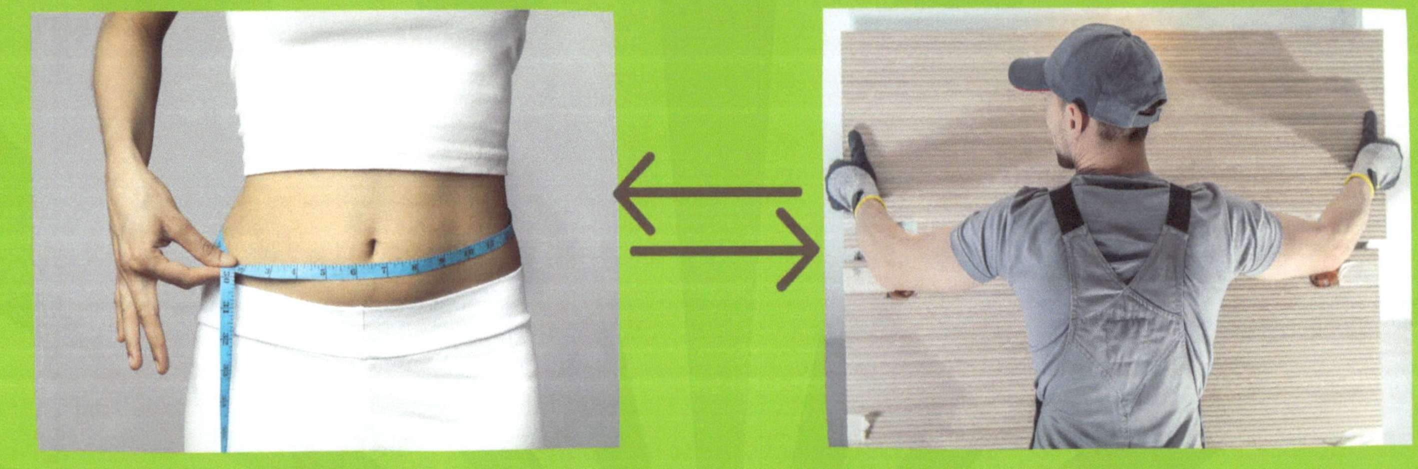

thin

prim

large

gran

easy

fàcil

difficult

difícil

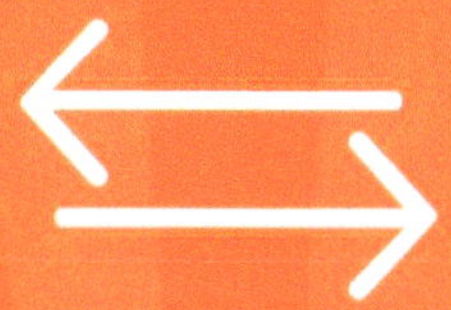

stand up

aixecar-se

sit down

seure

sweet

dolç

salty

salat

heavy

pesat

light

lleuger

in

dins

out

fora

dirty

brut

clean

net

close

tancat

open

obert

pencils

llapis

clock

rellotge

key

clau

book

llibre

bed

llit

crib

bressol

table

taula

chair

cadira

car

cotxe

bike

bicicleta

plane

avió

boat

vaixell

train

tren

helicopter

helicòpter

firetruck

camió de bombers

firefighter

bomber

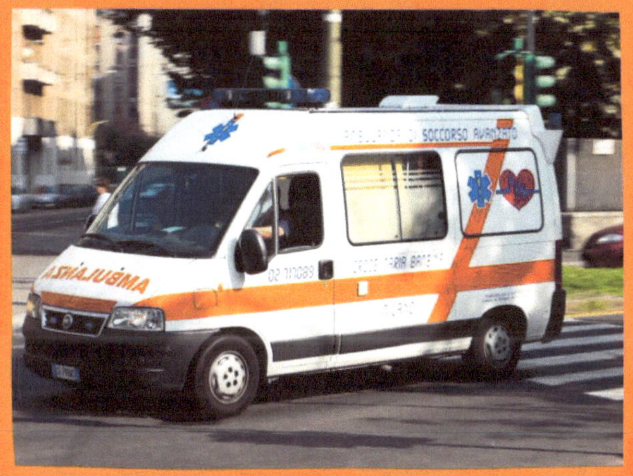

ambulance

ambulància

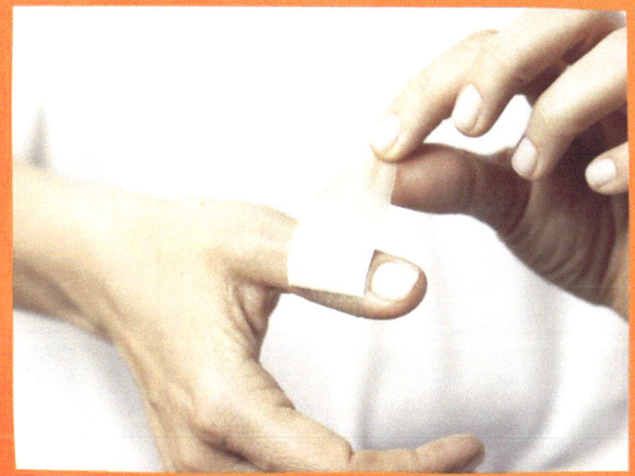

bandage

embenatge

paramedic

paramèdic

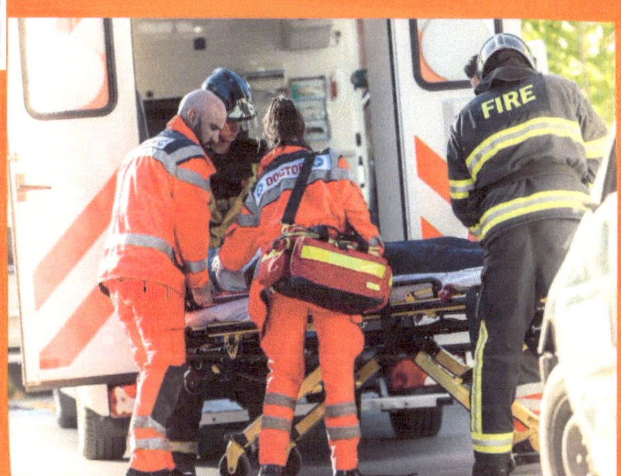

rescue team

equip de rescat

forest

bosc

mountain

muntanya

grass

herba

sand

sorra

tree

arbre

flower

flor

butterfly

papallona

ant

formiga

cat

gat

dog

gos

horse

cavall

mouse

ratolí

cow

vaca

pig

porc

sheep

ovella

duck

ànec

goose

oca

rabbit

conill

fish

peix

vet

veterinari

doctor

doctor

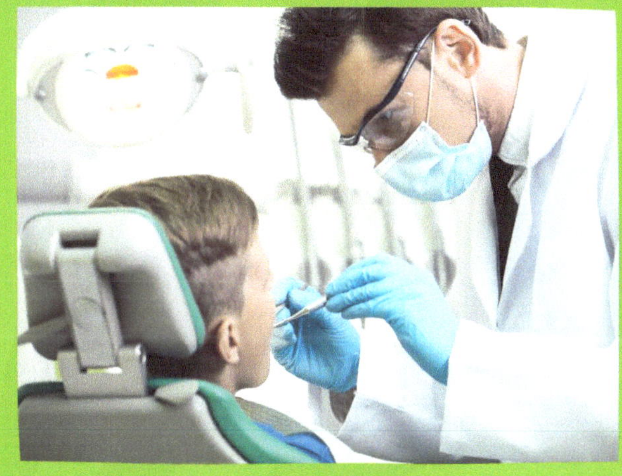

dentist

dentista

pharmacist

farmacèutic

nurse

infermera

head

cap

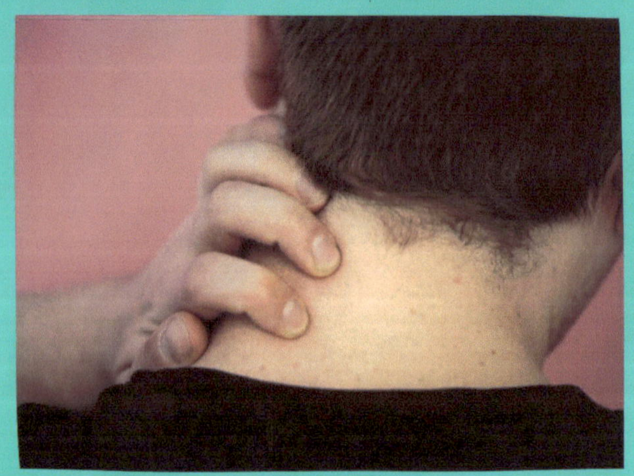

neck

coll

foot

peu

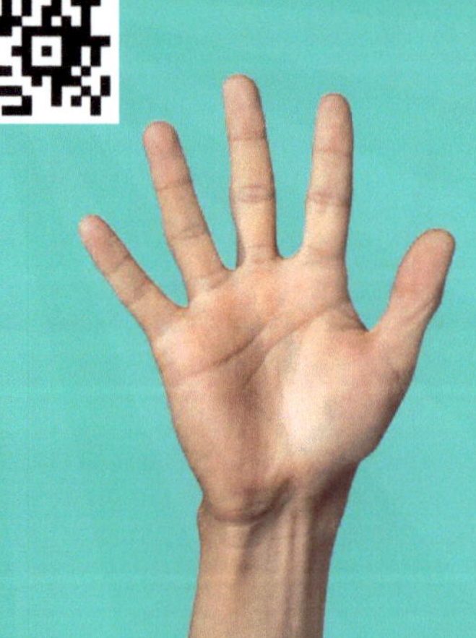

hand

mà

teeth

dents

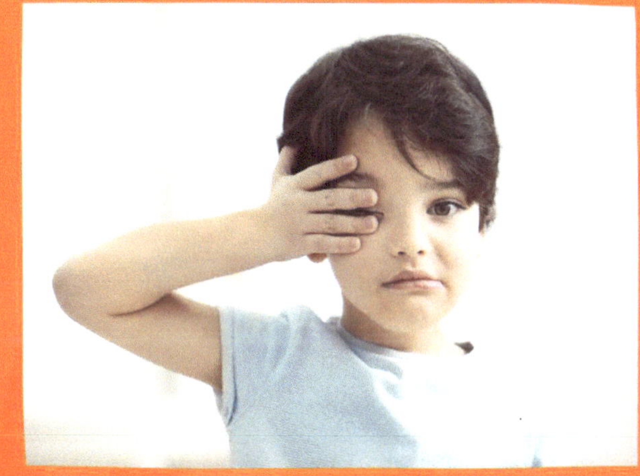

eye

ull

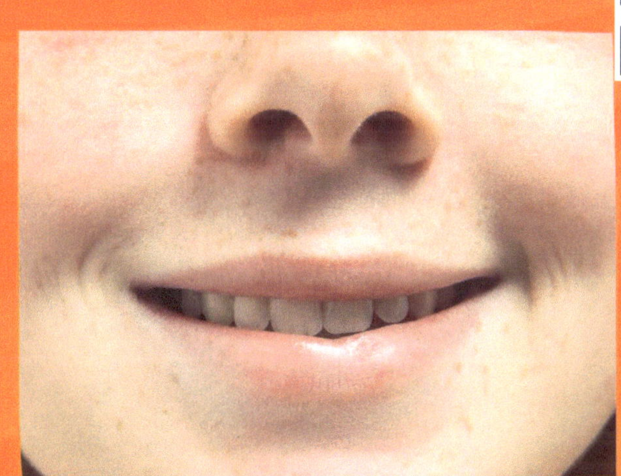

mouth

boca

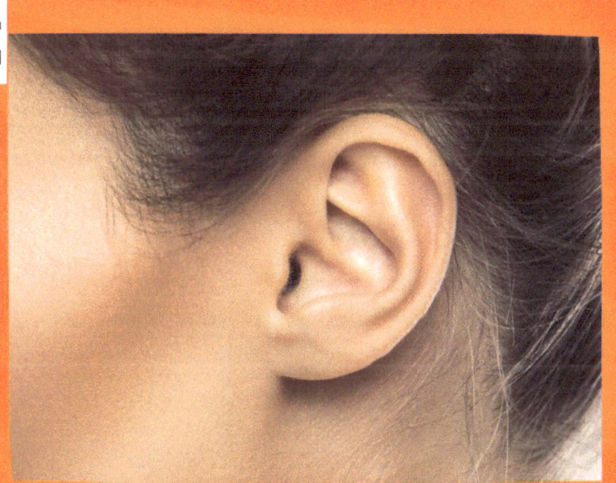

ear

orella

hat

barret

dress

vestit

pants

pantalons

shoes

sabates

coat

abric

scarf

bufanda

umbrella

paraigua

glasses

ulleres

sun

sol

cloudy

ennuvolat

rainy

plujós

moon

lluna